MY FIRST 50

KIM EVOY BRYANT

WESTBOW
PRESS®
A DIVISION OF THOMAS NELSON
& ZONDERVAN

WestBow Press books may be ordered through
booksellers or by contacting:

WestBow Press
A Division of Thomas Nelson & Zondervan
1663 Liberty Drive
Bloomington, IN 47403
www.westbowpress.com
1 (866) 928-1240

ISBN: 978-1-5127-5965-5 (sc)
ISBN: 978-1-5127-5967-9 (hc)
ISBN: 978-1-5127-5966-2 (e)

Library of Congress Control Number: 2016916715

Print information available on the last page.

WestBow Press rev. date: 10/13/2016

Dedication

For Jocelyn, Sydney and Houston

CONTENTS

FORWARD

· ·

Thoughts on Love, Loyalty and Legacy
by Lauren Evoy Davis

Jesus' message is all about love — but he never married. When we think about love these days, it's often Hallmark-inspired romantic love. But real love us so much deeper and more powerful. And — spoiler alert— it's all you need. Do you have a friend who you have known since childhood? Or a sibling? If you do, you know what Jesus is talking about. That unconditional loyal love of giving a friend a Band-aid when they fall off their bike, of standing up to bullies, of making that phone call to check-in after a break-up or job loss or funeral. It's called agape love from the Greek for "the highest form of love." Do you ever get a phone call from someone you have known for years and you say, "I was just thinking about you!" Here's why: Love endures. It reminds to be less self-focused and more concerned of others. Mostly, it heals.

Is it easy to love and be loved? No, not always. But, even when we're not lovable, someone out there still loves us. I choose the serenity prayer when I'm feeling uncharitable towards my fellow humans: "God, grant me the serenity to accept the things I cannot change, to change the things I can, and the wisdom to know the difference." This prayer is commonly known in addiction circles but it really applies to everyday life—cranky children, jerky drivers, and that weird person in line trying to pick a fight with the clerk and draw you into their tirade about the sales price of cantaloupe.

Love is a gift, and primarily what this book is about. If you have a relationship with God you realize that He put these imperfect, funny, and loving people into our lives for a reason. Well, for one reason, you can't hug God. But you can hug humans and puppies. Fish, not so much. This book will enable you to learn the history of where you originated and why you have long toes, love Triscuits, and a keep a collection of wacky Christmas movies. Is love always easy? No, but it encourages us to be brave. Here's another saying I love and later on in this book you will see, Kim's message really embodies. It's from Ann Voskamp, a mama and writer on spirituality. "Be Brave. Do not pray for the hard thing to go away. But pray for the bravery to come that's bigger than the hard thing." I'll end with how my friend Pastor Faith Lewis ends her weekly message. "Pray about everything, worry about nothing, walk in faith, and find a friend for the journey. For we are blessed in order to be a blessing."

I have been blessed and Kim is my friend for the journey. Be blessed by this work of enduring love for you.

INTRO

· ·

It's hard for me to believe that in just a few weeks I will be 50 years old. I remember in the 80's saying that when the year 2000 came around, I would be 35, and how old that seemed. Now it is 2014 – I guess I really didn't think past age 35.

At 50 now I am looking back and looking forward. What have I accomplished, is anything that I have done lasting, will anyone remember me 50 years from now. And I've come to the conclusion that what matters is not me. What matters is that I pass on the legacy, the gift that I've been given by those who lived before, to the generations to come.

In the last few months I've been working on Ancestry. com. Besides confirming what I know about our Czech, Slovak. English, Irish, and Welsh ancestry, I also learned that we may have Greek and Italian ancestors, among others, which explains why we tan easily. After watching the show "Who do you think you are," I was sure that we must be related to royalty, good leaders, maybe even Elvis. The web site is great in detailing births, deaths, marriages, children and other data gathered from government records, military records and some details that folks remember that may not have been recorded. But the most important things are missing from this list of records. Exactly "who" were our ancestors and what have they passed on to us?

I've been thinking a lot about legacy since Dad's death last year. I've been thinking about my place in the world and how I even got here in the first place. About how I got through school, through college and different jobs, why marriage and children have been so important, why I value family and friends and community, and how and why God has become number one in my life. None of this happens by accident. Generations of people since the beginning of time had to come together to the point where I was even put on this earth.

So, when I thought about my children, Jocelyn, Sydney and Houston, I wanted to put these thoughts and lessons down on paper so that they could pass on what I have learned. Although I won't always be around, I wanted the lessons that I learned from my parents and they learned from their parents to carry on. And not just lessons good stories and some history about how my mother's family came from Czechoslovakia, how my father's family came from England, how we started out in Pennsylvania and New Jersey and have migrated south. I wanted my children to know my parents, to know about my grandparents and to know about Mimi, my grandmother who has just celebrated 100 years on this earth.

I hope that you'll find this book interesting, funny and helpful when moving forward in your own lives. I hope that you'll see the hand of God in each aspect of my life (even when I wasn't paying attention.) The legacy of our family now lies in you. Pass it on.

1

CHILDHOOD AND CHILDREN

● ●

I knew from the very beginning that I would have children in my life. And having children has been the absolute best part of my life—watching them grow and seeing things through their eyes. My first granddaughter has just come into my life, and I am so excited to start this process again and again. It takes me back to my own childhood.

MY CHILDHOOD

Memories from childhood can be the most vibrant. One of my first memories is of my grandfather's house in Stone Harbor on the water. Pop Pop's house was the third one on the left as you crossed over the bridge. He had a boat dock with three boats. The dock had several levels: one for sitting and enjoying the scenery, one for cleaning fish, and a floating dock, which was my favorite. I can still remember the breeze in the summertime, the sound of the other boats going by, the salty aroma of the water, and watching the bridge rise and fall when the big boats passed by. But the part I remember like it was yesterday was swimming there. My mother would put on my big orange life preserver (this was in the late 1960s), and then she would tie one end of a rope to the dock and the other end to the life preserver. Because the current was so strong, I was not able to swim against it. But I would jump in from the floating dock, float as far as the rope would take me, and pull myself back. I did this again and again. When

I got tired, I would get back on the floating dock and lay there in the sun, sometimes falling asleep. To this day when I am trying to relax, I think of that floating dock and how I would dry off in the warm sun, and it almost seems like I am back in Stone Harbor. What a great memory.

Although I never met my Mom's mother, Pauline Jackson, I learned that she was a top roller skater, and she later helped run Pop Pop's roller skating rink in Philadelphia. Maybe that's how I learned to love skating, but of another type—on the ice.

Another memory takes me to ice-skating on our pond in January. My parents had a funeral home that was designed by my grandmother Dorothy Miriam Stratford Evoy. Friends called her Dottie. We called her Mimi. Built in 1975, Evoy Funeral Home stands today as a beautiful two-story Southern-style white building with big Doric columns outlining the front porch. But in the massive front yard is a pond. The pond used to freeze over in the winter, and our house became the place for ice-skating, ice hockey, hot chocolate, and chili. Mom had a box of ice skates on the back porch that included our skates plus those left there by folks over the years. I can't remember a time that we did not have enough skates for anyone who wanted to have fun. I can remember being on the school bus coming home from school, and when I saw the little kids who were already home skating, my heart would race— since I knew I could not get on that ice fast enough! Without taking off my coat, I would drop my books and get on my skates. I always wanted ice hockey skates like my brothers had, but Mom said girls should wear figure skates. That didn't stop me from having my own hockey stick. I still have a pretty good slap shot. Along with friends from the neighborhood, my brothers and I would be at the pond daily for as long as it was frozen. We all took turns cleaning the ice with snow shovels. And when it got dark, Dad would put the light on; we would play music from the record player through the outdoor speakers that he installed to play Christmas music. Times like these were, and still are, magical.

MY CHILDREN

I think that my children are great and funny. They're my kids, so of course I feel that way. I see so many funny things about them. Here are a few.

- One wore panty hose over pants and under shoes, at age three.
- One wrote on furniture with cheese.
- One made great, funny greeting cards—a birthday card had my big head glued on to a little, tiny, magazine-lady body.
- One loves to give "as seen on TV" gifts, such as the Pocket Hose, Bacon Bowls, and the Easy View Glare Blocker.
- One had a "history" dance any time we made plans to see historical sites in Virginia.

They all take funny pictures, tell great stories, and try to see the best in life. I'm proud of all of them and their willingness to try new things. They are all great travelers. They love music. And they are all a gift from God.

I cannot imagine my own life without children. And I say that realizing that this is not what everyone wants. For me, it has been a learning experience—one that has changed me and helped me to grow and mature. Responsibility can be taught, but children have motivated me to be responsible. Patience can be described, but being a parent has required a tremendous amount of practicing patience. Love was certainly given by my parents, but having children has shown me how to give love freely, unconditionally, and willingly. I can't wait to see what's in store for the next fifty years. I thank God for my children and now my grandchildren. He taught me these love lessons through them.

2

SISTERS

. . . .

MY SISTER

I can remember the day Mom told me she was going to have another baby. I was getting ready to turn eleven, and even though I already had three brothers, I was excited about a new baby in the family. As the time grew closer, I can remember praying, *Please be a girl, please be a girl.* The truth was that having brothers was not a bad thing. Almost all of the kids our age in the neighborhood were boys, and I was okay with playing ice hockey and having my own toy gun. To this day I still enjoy being with the boys, talking about farming, politics, business and hearing their jokes. But I really wanted a sister.

When Laurie was born in the spring of in 1976, even though I wasn't really a crier, I teared up. We were all excited about a new girl in the family, but now I had a sister. Little did I know what a huge and positive influence Laurie would have in my life.

Laurie and I are almost twelve years apart in age. The year that she went to kindergarten, I entered twelfth grade. We lived together for a short time in our parents' house, and we even shared a room. Looking back, I think that may be the reason we're so close now—we didn't grow up together. Over time, we became friends. The best of friends.

When Laurie graduated from college, she came to live with us for a short time. We even worked together. And that's when our friendship began. We started traveling together, sometimes just to and from New Jersey to see our folks. Other times we enjoyed longer trips. Our travels took us to England when I had a business trip and just wanted someone to travel with. And we had a great time finding out that we really enjoyed many of the same things—eating good food, visiting museums, and laughing hysterically when something went awry during our journey, which like clockwork, it always does. One of our memorable trips was coming back from New Jersey after Thanksgiving. Laurie and I were both feeling under the weather from a stomach bug, but I was doing a little better than she was. I went to get in the car, and Mom was helping Laurie with her suitcase. At that moment, Laurie was nauseous; she threw up on a tree in the front yard, and a little girl riding on a bike rode by and yelled to my mother, "Hello, Mrs. Evoy!" Did the child not see what was happening? It was like a movie. I start laughing, Laurie gets in the car, and off we go. We shared a small order of french fries and a Coke on the road. And then Laurie's car overheated on I-95. All we could do was crank up the heat to get the warmth away from the engine and laugh. Here we are almost twenty years since that incident, and we continue to travel together, now with our families. But what is it that draws us closer each year?

WE DECIDE WHAT MATTERS

Do Laurie and I ever disagree? Yes, we do. We have been on opposite sides of several topics, which for a while we shared on a blog called *Evoy vs. Evoy*—where we "promised to fight fair" and argued mostly about politics. But, this I know for sure. As we age and mature, our relationships grow, age, and mature. And things that used to be important—like winning an argument and bringing the other to your side of the debate—do not seem to matter anymore. In the last four years, we have lost both of our parents, a beloved uncle, and a grandmother. We have dealt head-on with long-term illness in our family and with situations that seemed impossible to believe. There have been difficult trials and emotional pain. And I am so thankful that I had my sister to walk hand in hand with me, literally, through these times. Mom used to call us the "twins born twelve years apart." This became apparent when we would simultaneously perform the same movement, such as enacting a plane's turbulence during a game of Pictionary. How do we do the same things when we really didn't grow up together? Dad used to call us "the bookends." What has been, I think, so extraordinary, is how we work together during these difficult times. When I am weak, Laurie picks up where I cannot move forward. When Laurie needs help, I somehow have the strength to do the next thing. We seem to move in perfect harmony during the darkest hours of our life.

WE KEEP LAUGHING

Thankfully we have managed to keep our sense of humor intact. We almost always have a funny story to tell or a memory of some hilarity that took place when we are together. Laurie likes to remind me of the time that I gave her a perm, but only on the top of her head. She also laughs heartily every time someone asks if I'm her mother. I thought she would fall over when someone asked if I was Mom's sister. Okay, so I dress a little on the conservative side. It could be worse.

WE WORK TOGETHER

Being the big sister and properly telling others what to do, as is my position as the eldest of five, I have made many suggestions to Laurie about how to proceed in life. Laurie has to be credited for hearing all of my crazy ideas, never seemingly to tire of any business idea that pops into my head. Even if she suffers some of the unfortunate consequences. We've already covered my "how to save money by doing our own hair" ideas. But I have taken it to the next step. One time I thought that we could make money creating pottery, and convinced Laurie and her husband to buy a kiln. It was never used because Laurie was afraid of the type of electrical hook-up would be required to support this type of equipment and because she's already had two fires—one in Aunt Marty's kitchen making toast and another when she baked her first cheesecake in a very old oven. They sold the kiln on Craig's List. Then, I thought I would help her save money by power washing their back deck at her townhouse in Alexandria, Va. Unfortunately I didn't take into consideration that the extreme water pressure would remove some of the deck finish, causing the end result to look like a humongous child with a monster-sized crayon wrote all over the deck. I love my brother-in-law, but especially because he has not yet disowned me over the "great ideas." I have started a craft business. Hopefully Laurie won't suffer any glue mishaps or sewing gone awry. She'll probably stick with collages or sock puppets.

FRIENDS + SISTERS-IN-LAW = LIFE-LONG SISTERS

During my first 50 years, I have been blessed with not only having a sister, but also friends who I consider as close as sisters. My sisters-in-law have been some of my closest friends. And I've been blessed throughout my lifetime with friends that are like sisters, from grade school to college to those in my adult life. But what exactly makes a good friend a life-long sister? My friends have been very supportive during difficult times. We also enjoy laughing when we're together. However, the thing that brings me closest to them is honesty. My friends, true friends, have always been completely honest with me. There are always challenges in life, everyone has them. There are times when I have felt sorry for myself for different things. So, I seek wise council, my friends. Because they love me, in order for them to lift me up without tearing me down, they have been honest in their responses to any problem or issue I bring to them. A true friend wants what is best for you. And while hearing the truth may not be the salve you were hoping for on what appears to be an open wound, a friend can see the big picture and help to lead you in the right direction. What's great about being 50 is that you have so many situations to look back on and see how your friends help to bring you through a difficult time and then not dwell on it, but together move forward. I am fortunate, blessed and do not deserve the greatest friendships with my sister and life-long sisters that anyone could want.

3
WHY NOT ME?

. . . .

When things happen in life that do not necessarily go our way, we tend to ask "why me?" But I had an experience that was a turning point and had me asking "why not me?"

Children have been the best part of my life and with my third, I was just as excited as I was with the first two. Houston was born in February, during a very snowy winter. I was 40 and complaining that I was heavy, tired, and out of breath but, maybe because I was 40 and pregnant. *Get in line behind the rest of the 40 year old and pregnant ladies and stop your whining.* Even the doctor thought the same, so it was no real news to him. In the early morning of February 22, we went to the hospital and by 11:30am Houston came into the world. It was the fastest delivery that I had, the girls had been a good 12 hours each. Since Jocelyn could drive, I sent the girls to school, no worries. I cried with joy, we made phone calls, and had a few of Houston's first visitors. Dave left after dinner to take the girls home and I was ready to sleep a bit. But by 9:30pm, things changed. Actually, *everything* changed.

I didn't know what it was, but my blood pressure was so high that I had to be moved to another floor of the hospital and began medication to try and control it. For the last few weeks of my pregnancy, I was having shortness of breath, but didn't think much of it. I coughed so much during labor and delivery that they gave me Robitussin. (Being the smarty that I was, I took Vicks Vapor Rub to the hospital thinking that this would be helpful. The cardiologist didn't think so). The pulmonary doctor started me on breathing treatments, but they did not have much effect on my breathing. Houston was born on a Tuesday and by Friday they started me on tests. The pulmonary doctor drained fluid from one of my lungs to give me some relief and assist with breathing, which helped. I had tests, scans and x-rays all day Friday. And at the end of the day we met with the cardiologist.

PPCM – peripartum cardiomyopathy was the diagnosis. This condition was extremely rare and I did not fit the description of the women who have this sometimes fatal condition. It could be treatable, but we also read and the doctor confirmed that the fatality rate for PPCM women was 40% to 50%. I didn't sleep for at least of 48 hours. I could not get my brain around this. Dave and I had just celebrated our 1st wedding anniversary in October. Did God bring us this far for Dave to be a single father? Would my girls be left without a mother during the challenging teen years? Would Houston and

I even have the opportunity to know each other? I just didn't get it. At night I laid in bed and thought about all that we had been told, the fact that Houston was healthy and I wasn't, what would the future bring. It was one of those few times in life when you have come to the end of the rope and the only option is to depend completely on God. And I did.

As I look back, I didn't cry about this diagnosis. I was so taken back, not prepared to hear that I had a heart condition. We even questioned why I would be meeting with a cardiologist at first. This was something that I never heard of and a condition that could not be diagnosed until after delivery. It was brought on by the pregnancy and began to shut down the left ventricle of my heart, very similar to congestive heart failure. When I laid down I could not breathe. This is what caused the fluid build-up in my body. Immediately the doctor prescribed drugs to help support my heart while it healed and other drugs to help rid my body of the fluids. During the next 3 weeks I lost 50 pounds, baby and fluid and as a sort of kind consequence, back in my pre-maternity clothes.

I could not have gotten through this without God and my husband. Dave was by my side during delivery, during the tests, during the diagnosis. Dave has a great strength and steadiness in difficult times, able to see the facts, able to work toward a good solution. He came to the hospital every day. On Saturday morning (after the Friday diagnosis and no sleep for the previous two days), I was sitting in a chair holding Houston. Because I was so weak, a nurse had to move me from the bed to the chair and then place Houston in my arms. I was too weak to pick him up. The nurse told me that Houston was doing so well that they would be releasing him today. But not me. I fell apart. I feel the way you do when it seems your world has spun out of control and there is no turning back. I called Dave. He was already up and said he was coming to the hospital and said that it would all be okay. And that part was. Even though my mother-in-law showed up at the hospital with a baby seat and determination, Dave said that he would take Houston home that night. And the next day Dave and Houston came back to the hospital, sleepy and in the same clothes (Houston, not Dave) but fed and okay.

My heart did heal. By summer we camped with family and I water skied. It felt great to be healthy and living life. And then guilt set in.

As I read more articles about PPCM, my heart broke for these young women who would unknowingly give their lives for their babies, leaving their husbands to start this family on their own. Why not me? A good friend lost his battle with cancer that year. He deserved to live a long life – he was a much better person that I was, good father, husband, friend. Why not me? Another friend lost her battle with cancer leaving her husband and children, a strong Christian that others could look up to. Why not me? I felt guilty for surviving. Looking back I always have to remind myself that God has a plan. God always has a plan. His plan was fulfilled for others, and his plan for me is still in motion.

Romans 8:28 New International Version (NIV)
28 And we know that in all things God works for the good of those who love him, who have been called according to his purpose.

It's true that God puts you on a path and prepares you for what is coming. And what came required strength, the kind that you can't read about or do on your own. I know now that although there were things that happened in my life up until that time that were unfortunate, I had not suffered tragedy or pain the way others do. When Dave required three heart procedures, I needed strength to be there for him the way he had been there for me. When Mom became ill and was hospitalized, I needed strength to be there for her and Dad. When Mom passed away, I needed strength to be supportive for Dad. When Dad had hernia surgery, I needed strength and a good sense of humor to help

Dad through healing. And when Dad became and ill and died suddenly, I needed strength to get up the next morning. God pointed out so many things during difficult times, but one of the most important was the focus on others. And then God blessed me with good things that also came along.

Jocelyn got married, Sydney graduated from high school, Houston scored his first goal in soccer and made his profession of faith and God allowed me the privilege of being right there with each of them. I'm changing my tune now. God has shown me so much now, pointed out what is important like working on running toward relationships rather than away from them. I don't know what God has in store for me in the future, but I am confident that "wherever He leads I'll go".[1]

---

[1] Baptist Hymnal, Author: Baylus Benjamin McKinney

4

DEATH STINKS – PART 1

I always assumed that both of my parents would live well into their 90's. Mom's grandmother and aunts had lived into their 80's and Dad's mother was still living at 97. As a matter of fact, all of my grandmother's siblings had lived into their 80's and 90's, and my grandmother did indeed live to be 100. So when Mom got sick, I really believed that this was just a bump in the road of life, not the end of it.

During Easter break of 2011, I took the kids to Cape May for a visit with my parents. Mom seemed very tired, but not necessarily sick. She just seemed worn out, but I had no idea what would be coming. I spoke with my parents weekly and periodically emailed, but always had a pretty good idea about what was going on. In June, Mom had a tooth infection that really seemed to take over her body. She went to the doctor, started taking antibiotics and we thought that was the end of it.

Dave and I were getting back from Costa Rica. We were there celebrating a friend's wedding and it was the first time in a long while that we had a chance to travel, just the 2 of us. We enjoyed beautiful weather, good food, sleeping in, getting some sun and really felt refreshed. I now feel that God was getting us ready for what was to come. We flew into Atlanta and I called Mom and Dad to let them know we were close to home and also to wish Dad a happy father's day. But things were not good. Mom was getting weaker and starting to have difficulty breathing. She refused to go to the doctor, but

I told them I would be there as soon as possible and she would have to see someone. The next day Dad took her to the doctor and then to the emergency room.

Laurie and I are good travelers together, so we made a plan the next day and headed to NJ on Tuesday. The doctors were taking tests and trying to find out what was going on. When we arrived at the hospital, Mom was indeed struggling with her breathing and she also had large bumps on her face. I thought maybe she had some sort of infection. Mom was sitting up in a chair and making jokes about us getting involved in her business. "You two," she said, still able to roll her eyes and make jokes. Because of that, we didn't consider that this was life threatening.

By Wednesday, Laurie and I took turns going to the hospital with Dad so that the kids could stay at home and enjoy the pool. I just happened to be the one that was there when the diagnosis came. Mom was in bed and awake, but had no energy. The doctor sat us down and discussed what was going on. Although they were waiting for all tests to come in, he believed that Mom had Non-Hodgkin's lymphoma, a very aggressive, fast moving cancer. When Laurie and I were both at the hospital, we all discussed the next step. Mom could be treated close to home, but the doctor felt that another hospital in Philadelphia would be better suited for her type of lymphoma and we should consider moving her as soon as possible. Phone calls were made, we settled on a decision and within hours Mom was moved. She would never return to Cape May or her home.

Within 24 hours of Mom arriving at the new hospital, the doctors felt that she needed to be on a ventilator and ultimately dialysis. Fluid was building up in her body and had to be removed in order to assist her breathing. In a few days Mom would receive her first chemotherapy treatment, and would be sedated for the next month.

I always said that while there were some things in my life that weren't great and wish they had not happened, we as a family had not suffered tragedy. When elder relatives passed away after long well-lived lives, I had a "circle of life" philosophy, but not this time. When I stood in the hospital, I felt God giving me the strength to move forward. Something occurred to me that had to come from God — this situation was not about me. We had to be laser focused on Mom and her treatment, supportive of Dad and making sure that he stayed healthy and needed to communicate with family and friends about Mom's progress. It is very difficult for me to see anyone in pain, physical or emotional, and God gave me the desire to comfort wherever I could. God showed us that we are not in charge — of anything! My prayer life changed dramatically from praying about certain circumstances, to praying for His will and our strength, no matter what the outcome.

In July, Mom woke up in a Philadelphia hospital ICU and we explained what had taken place, what she had been through, that a month had passed and that she was making progress. She was shocked. While she rested, we heard July 4th fireworks from a nearby hotel. She was weak but alert, and it was so good to see her awake. Soon she was breathing on her own again. Mom usually disliked hospitals but she was a model patient, always kind to the staff and proud to introduce her visitors. After getting off the ventilator to breathe on her own, her first words were "ice water" — a treat from the nurses. During the next 5 months, Mom would go from ICU to a rehab facility and then back to the hospital. There would be multiple rounds of chemotherapy and physical therapy She lost her hair and gained her strength. We were hopeful and starting to discuss her coming home. The hospital had much better food and she reluctantly went back to the rehab one time, but first asked if it could be after dinner. We laughed, but she was serious.

Laurie remembers Mom in good spirits for her birthday in November. The chef delivered a birthday cake he baked just for her and she was delighted. Mom, being an only child, never had to share a room, so it was funny to see her get annoyed with her chatty roommate who was recovering from knee surgery. When that lady left, Mom was relieved!

December was a great visit for all of us. Mom was in the rehab facility, so we took some holiday costume jewelry and new clothes so that she could feel fancy during the holiday. She loved it! We talked and laughed and made plans for when Mom was coming home, probably January.

In mid-January, something happened and we're still not entirely sure what it was. Mom's health was deteriorating. It appeared that an infection was invading her already weakened system. Also, the oncologist discussed that there may have been a third type of cancer. Mom had been fighting 2-types of lymphoma, known as double-hit. Her system was passed the point of no return. She had fought a difficult battle. The doctor called to tell us the news and that we should come to the hospital in the next day or so. Laurie and I left the next day, Tuesday, and were with Mom that evening, she was alert, asked for a sip of Coke. The next morning Mom pulled her oxygen mask to the side and uttered her last word, "home". Then she closed her eyes and began to rest peacefully. She looked more comfortable than she had in months.

We stayed with Dad, visiting at the hospital. Our brothers came, close friends and relatives. Instead of discussing sad things, we talked about good things so that Mom could hear, like we were around a Thanksgiving table. Laurie played some of Mom's favorite music like swing bands and also Simon and Garfunkle. A friend brought a soothing blanket. We described the window that Mom looked out of daily from our home, the pond, the ducks, cherry blossoms and weeping willow tree. Nothing prepares you for these moments, but God gives us the comfort we need to comfort others. I know that all of this came from Him.

By Friday evening, Laurie, Dad, brother Bill and I went out to dinner and then back to the hospital. Mom had been in ICU since Monday. We returned to the hospital room and had the television sound on low and rested. At about 9pm, we saw that there was a change in Mom's breathing. It appeared to all of this that she may be slipping away now. So we all stood around the bed, held her hands and began to comfort her by talking about something that we loved – being in a boat on the ocean. We all took part in describing the boat, the feel of the waves, the smell of the ocean, the feel of the breeze, the warmth of the sun. We talked about Mom reeling in a fish, which she loved to do. And within a few short moments and a one deep breath, Mom was gone, to eternity.

Over the next few hours and days, we made phone calls and plans for Mom's funeral. The service and the minister were comforting, talking about Mom and singing her favorite hymns. I kept saying to myself,

1 Corinthians 15:55

"Oh death where is thy sting, oh

grave where is thy victory."

Instead of sitting alone during the visitation, I wanted to reach out to everyone who knew and loved Mom. I wanted to be there for family and also for her friends. One of her friends said "I'm so sorry for you" and I responded "I'm so sorry for you." Again, God placed on my heart that this was now about Mom and going forward with Dad. But I was certainly not the only one in mourning, I was not special and did not require special treatment. When God places that on your heart, it comes naturally to want to comfort others. And in doing so, my heart began to heal.

We don't know why Mom and Dad had to suffer for so long during this illness, but if I had to guess, it was to remind Mom about how much she was loved by so many. She even commented about how many cards she had received during her stay in the hospital and the rehabilitation center. And of course we never left her without saying "I love you."

5

DEATH STINKS – PART 2

· ·

We were still tan from Dad's wedding. It was unbelievable that we were standing at the foot of his bed in ICU 3 weeks after he took a leap of faith to remarry, watching him slowly slip away. This scene was way too familiar, as we were in the same place, different hospital with Mom, and it hadn't even been 2 years.

Mom was ill in the spring of 2011. For me personally, I had already spent more time in hospitals that I would like, but thankfully with good results. Dave had undergone 3 heart ablations at 3 different hospitals in 6 months, the last one in February of this same year. But in June, Mom was very sick. Dad took her to the local hospital and in the next 3 days the course of all of our lives shifted. Mom was diagnosed with B-cell, Non-Hodgkins lymphoma also known as double hit, where patients have mutations on two significant genes, where most lymphoma patients have a mutation on only one. She already had tumors throughout her body at stage IV. The doctors at the local hospital recommended that we send her to a hospital in Philadelphia and that is what we did that same day. Within 24 hours, Mom required intubation and was placed in the bone marrow ICU. She was unconscious for the next 30 days.

After the first month Mom had successfully undergone the first round of chemotherapy. The next step was another round of chemotherapy and then talk of a rehabilitation center. For the next 5 months, Mom would be back and forth between the hospital and the rehabilitation center, fighting infections and then getting stronger. By December we were visiting with her, laughing, starting to enjoy the Christmas holiday and talking about her homecoming in January. Dad labored to make the house ready for Mom and kept the Christmas tree up for her to enjoy. But things in our lives can change in a minute.

Dad suffered terribly with Mom's passing. I would have done anything had it been in my power to take away his pain. In the summer of 2012 when Dad told us that he was spending time with a new lady in his life, I was very happy for him. Marie had been a friend of our family for many years, and she knew all too well the pain of losing a spouse too early in life. Marie and Dad were a good match. They were engaged by Christmas and planned a wedding in the fall of 2013.

October came, so we packed our bags and headed to Punta Cana, Dominican Republic for the wedding. Dad looked tired, but I figured that it was stress from the wedding, getting the house ready for sale, etc. The wedding was a very meaningful time. And while I missed Mom and wished that she could still be with us, this was what was best for Dad and Marie. They both deserved happiness and peace. We had a fun time and glad we could be there to share their day.

A week later, Dad and Marie came home on Friday. On Monday Marie called to tell me that Dad was in the hospital, possibly with Lyme disease. We didn't worry at first because Dad was healthier that a lot of men his age, hitting the gym at least 4 times a week. But when he did not respond to medication, he too was sent to a hospital in Philadelphia. Dad was getting weaker by the day. And when the final diagnosis came it was Hemophagocytic Lymphohistiocytosis (HLH). His immune system was a raging storm in his body, attacking his organs and eventually shutting down his body. We prayed for him and with him. Dad and Marie's minister anointed him with oil and prayed for him. People up and down the east coast prayed for him. But God had other plans. When all of the options for saving Dad were exhausted, we gathered around him, told him how much he was loved, played Christmas music and held his hand as he left this earth and went to his eternal life. It seemed unbelievably unfair. So to remind Dad that his life was important, I made him a promise to carry on his legacy and all the things that he had taught us.

As much as death stinks, so does making funeral arrangements. We want to represent our loved ones in the best way possible, but once they're gone, it is hard to do anything that seems to matter. I decided to share Dad's legacy at his funeral. Mom and Dad sent us to church, taught us to thank God for our blessings and encouraged us to keep God in our lives. So that's what I talked about, Dad's love of God, family and country, and in that order. But the thought about why God would take Dad at this time, after he suffered so much with Mom's passing and then to begin finding joy in his new life with Marie was baffling. We did not understand. We were angry, not at God, but at the situation. At the funeral I talked about Dad representing the fruit of the spirit in his life: love, joy, peace, patience, kindness, goodness, faithfulness, gentleness, and self-control (Galatians 5:22-23). I said that we could see all of these things in his actions, that he did not just talk about things, he lived them.

For months I could not see the reason for Dad's death. And then one day it dawned on me; Dad had fulfilled the fruit of the spirit. Dad had fulfilled God's plan for him on this earth. It wasn't for me to say that Dad was taken too soon. I have to trust that this was God's plan. And I'm trusting God to heal the rest of us still here. Especially Marie.

The blessing that came from Dad's death was my relationship with Marie. We now have a strong bond because of the time that we spent together, hours of learning about each other and praying for and with Dad. Spending time with Marie now helps me to feel closer to Dad.

The result of living through the extended illness and death of loved ones has certainly been that of change. I am stronger and realize that with God, I am capable of many things.

Philippians 4:13
*"I can do all this through Him
who gives me strength."*

He has strengthened me, He has humbled me. He has given me a more positive perspective on anyone I meet during the day. He has caused me to not question how to serve Him, just to serve Him. He has made me appreciate each day with Dave, my children and as of last week, my new granddaughter. He has made me thankful. And He reminds me daily of the great reunion that we will have with Mom and Dad in eternity. I'm looking forward to it because I have so much to tell them.

6

SHOULD GRANDMA
WEAR BOOTY SHORTS

• •

Why is it that we always want to be something that we're not? Children always want to be older, adults always want to be younger, people want to be other people. I can remember being a young teen, 14, 15 and wanting so desperately to drive. I wanted to work, have my own money, learn to be independent. When I turned 30 I wanted to be 20 again. Life just seemed to go way too fast and I wanted to be carefree, make better decisions, go back and get another college degree.

Why couldn't I just be happy where I was? The truth was, I was probably comfortable with my age but not comfortable with who I was.

In my 30's I worked with a lady who had 3 children, one teen, one getting ready to be a teen and an adolescent. I had always heard folks making jokes about raising teens and how difficult it was going to be. When I teased this lady about escaping her home during the teen years, she said that she was looking forward to it. What??? What could you possibly be looking forward to??? She said that each stage of her children's lives had something to offer, they saw things with different perspectives and she was so glad to be there during each stage. Turns out that I was the one who wasn't acting my age. I already had two children and may have been missing something great in their lives. Raising children is not easy, and each stage is different, but the truth for my life is that having children has been the best part of my life. Maybe that's why they are spread out so far? I had one in my 20's, one in my 30's and one in my 40's. I told my husband that the next one would kill me.

We have to let children be children and enjoy each age and stage. This is something that seems to be passing away in this generation. I see children seemingly skipping childhood and losing their innocence much too early. Innocence about playing, innocence about make believe and just enjoying being a child. It's not my job to place blame, but I would caution parents to help maintain their childrens' innocence until they are ready for the world. Maybe holding off adult activities like cell phones, make-up, seductive clothing and providing age appropriate reading material and entertainment. At the other end of the childhood spectrum, we also need to make sure that when our children leave home, they leave as young adults, ready to be independent. It's okay for them to do their own laundry, manage finances etc. It's okay to let go, if taught properly, they will come back.

I haven't always been comfortable with me. There are times when I have not felt good enough in certain situations, felt guilty for past actions and words, not attractive physically or personally, and on and on. But can I tell you that at 50 it feels like I have arrived! I am finally comfortable in my own skin. At 50 I have put on a few pounds and still wear a bathing suit to the beach (one that covers up everything, no bikinis). At 50 I really do not want to be 18, hence the "no booty shorts" rule. I want to be 50 and I get to be 50. We've already lost several friends before their 50th birthday and so I see 50 as a gift. I've even gotten to the point where it's okay if someone asks if I'm Laurie's mother. Yes I say, don't I look good for my age?

My grandmother just turned 100. What's out there for me to do for the rest of my life? First I can continue parenting. I'm so glad that Houston is still home and that we have many years before he graduates from high school. I'm not saying that life is a breeze, but I still enjoy seeing life through his eyes and his excitement.

I like going places with him and Houston shouting out the make and model of each car on our ride from Virginia to New Jersey. I like hearing about his plans for life. And while Jocelyn and Sydney are off in the world each pressing forward in their own lives, I like hearing about what is happening, what's new. Our home time and holidays are now filled with much fun and laughter because we all really enjoy being together. And I enjoy working on the farm with Dave, my husband of 11 years. The farm is our interest, brings us mutual joy, the very best in us. The farm will be our earthly legacy, the one thing that we worked on together and where we will spend the rest of our lives.

My advice – have a birthday and wear your age with pride! Enjoy each stage of life. Enjoy each stage of your children's lives. I'll say it again, I get to be 50. I told my aunt that I was comfortable with moving to this age, I was comfortable with being 50. She said that's because you're not the one turning 75.

7

OUR FAMILY – CRAZY FUN

· ·

After living for 50 years, there would be far too many stories to put into one book. But I have attempted to put some of the stories that stand out for me. I'll tell about each person and just a few things.

MY GRANDMOTHER - TRAVELS WITH MIMI

It was August 2004, and Mimi was ready to go back to Florida. Usually she went in September, but when I told Mom that I could take Mimi, she said that August would be fine. The girls were out of school and Jocelyn just got her driver's license, so she would be able to do some of the driving back to Florida. So that was the plan, down and back in about 3 days. Or so we thought.

Mom and Dad brought Mimi to Virginia to stay one night and then we would get on our way. Dave and I were building a house, so we were living in a trailer on our new farm. We all enjoyed a had fried chicken al fresco (out of the heat of the trailer and in the shade of the pine trees) and then Mom and Dad headed back to the comfort of an inn in Charlottesville. We got Mimi settled for the night and finished our packing.

DAY 1

At about 8am, Jocelyn and I finished our breakfast, and packed up the Toyota 4-Runner. Mimi doesn't like to eat much when she travels, so she had a cup of tea and took her bag of snacks with her, and off we went. It was a nice day, about average heat for August and our destination was Brunswick, GA, which is a little more than halfway to Venice, FL from our house. There would be hotels and restaurants along the way, so no reservations necessary.

We stopped for lunch, and although Mimi was never hungry, she always had a little room for ice cream. By 6pm we were ready to stop, so in Brunswick, we found a restaurant for dinner. Jocelyn and I ordered pretty decent meals, and Mimi, due to her delicate condition (not sure what that was just yet), could only eat a hot fudge sundae. Again, not sure if that is exactly the doctor's recommendation, but Mimi was almost 90 and I wasn't going to argue. We found a nice, clean hotel and had a restful evening. Good thing.

DAY 2

If you've never been to Brunswick, GA or its' next door neighbor, Jeckyll Island, GA, you should visit. It is really lovely and defines different aspects of Georgia beaches. I know it's hot, but I just love the deep south and the moss that hangs from the trees and blows in the wind.

We got up, showered and dressed, and Jocelyn and I had a little breakfast in the hotel. Mimi brought her tea bag, so she was ready to go. There wasn't a rush or a schedule, so we all took our time and finally got back on I-95 south. Driving from Brunswick to Venice, FL is a relatively easy ride, we'd be there by dinner and could rest for the evening. Then we turned on the radio.

A tropical storm was already blowing through Florida, and we had pretty much missed that. But here came the hurricane that we thought would go away (or as I always say in my head, "it'll just burn off" as if it was a little, isolated storm). No, we were headed right into the eye. So it was time to think of plan B. Our trip would normally take us southwest through the center of Florida. But the storm was coming across the state and then toward northern Florida. There was no avoiding it.

We kept driving and listening to the radio. After a while, Jocelyn and I switched and she drove so that I could start making plans. I tried to talk with Mimi about the plans, but she was in disbelief about the storm and therefore wanted to ignore the facts that a hurricane was indeed on the way. I started to make a few telephone calls to see if we could get a hotel room somewhere off I-95 and by mid-afternoon. In order to be safe, we would have to have to get off the road before dinner, and I didn't want to wait out the hurricane in a car. Especially because things in our car started to get a little tense.

Mimi decided that she would do a little of the driving, from the back seat. That's what is needed in any tense situation. Around noon we started to get off of each exit to see if any hotels had vacancies, and they didn't. Everyone from the coast needed a room to escape the storm. Mimi saw a hotel that we had passed and ask Jocelyn to make a u-turn on the interstate. Okay, so that's illegal, but so what. I told Jocelyn to keep driving forward.

I said "Mimi, making a u-turn on the interstate is dangerous and it's against the law." and she firmly replied. "Well, I never heard that being against the law!"

And that was the first time, that under my breath I uttered words about not driving from the backseat. Then things got more tense, and worse.

Mimi kept it up for the next 2 hours, stating that we should just drive across the state and storm probably wouldn't be that bad. Except, who in the National Guard should I have called to ask if my Mimi could have access to Interstate 75, which they had just closed for the foreseeable future??? (I wish I could have recorded my blood pressure during this adventure).

Finally, at Ft. Pierce, we got off of I-95 and found a hotel. Mimi was so busy giving me directions about which room I should request, she failed to notice that in this sketchy part of town, the hotel shared a parking lot with a 2-story, fushia pink, adult bookstore called the Cosmic Kiss. It was so big and so loud that Jocelyn was laughing hysterically and asking me to take her photo next to the store, which being the responsible parent that I am, did. I got out of the car and headed to office to see if there was a room left and Mimi was still giving me directions about her room choices. Now I was uttering under my breath "you'll take what you get old woman."

I went to the front desk and they had one room left. The clerk who wasn't cleanly shaven and did not appear to be wearing a formal uniform or name tag, gave me a key to the room (was this 1950?) and I gave him cash in return. I could tell this would be a night to remember and decided not to share my credit card information with him.

We settled into our room, soon to discover that the sheets had not been changed and there were no clean towels. Back to the office and the clerk, who now appeared to be the only one employed there. Jocelyn and I went across the street to a diner to get some dinner, and Mimi agreed to eat a grilled cheese sandwich, which we brought back for her. The three of us quietly watched TV, tried not to touch anything, and proceeded to sleep with our clothes on. After the dirty sheet incident, we didn't want to come in contact with anything else.

We all dozed off for a while and then the madness really started. People were partying in the parking lot, knocking on our door and then kept turning the knob (Mimi had requested a ground floor room and that was exactly what we got). Unfortunately, because of the proximity to adult bookstore that must have been open 24 hours/day, folks were all over the place, in the storm, the rain and then wind, until the storm stopped and the sun came up. Finally.

DAY 3

I was ill. I was operating on no sleep and did I mention almost 40 and pregnant? We got up and got out. I was so happy to be back on the road, but not prepared for what we would see.

Florida is a very long state, and it is wider that you might think. So driving across the state would probably take a few hours, but we could make it. Except we weren't prepared to what we would see.

We started out west from Ft. Pierce, and after being on the road for a short while, saw the destruction that the storm had caused. Folks were in the streets, looking at the downed power lines and poles. Trailers where folks lived in the middle of the state were on their sides or upside down. The devastation was horrible. But we kept moving because at this point we had to get Mimi home. And I felt a little guilty for being so short tempered with her. So quietly, we weaved our way through the state, to Sarasota, and then south to Venice and finally made it there in the late afternoon. I walked through the door of the house, got a whiff of the moth balls and promptly threw up.

Bugs don't have a chance against Mimi. And when she leaves Florida, Mimi makes sure that no bugs are going to take over her home while she's gone. Hence the moth balls. They're everywhere, under the beds, in the closet, you name it. Mimi walked in the house like it was nothing. Everyone else has to stand outside until the whole place was aired out.

I will say this about Mimi – she has always been in her best element in Florida (or at least during my lifetime). Up north in New Jersey, she is fine. But when Mimi returns to her house in Florida, she is like a butterfly leaving the cocoon. One minute she is an elderly woman in the back seat of the car, and the next minute she is moving boxes from the house to the car and giving directions to anyone within earshot. I'm glad to see it and glad that we all survived the trip.

Mimi, like any good grandmother, has a few quirks. Some grandmothers have secret recipes. Mimi has a secret relationship with the UPS man. About once a week, he stops by and brings her a box. This all occurred to me once I regained my senses after opening the door. Mimi bought more dolls. I guess it was in the late 1980's, early 1990's that Mimi discovered Home Shopping Channel. What is more fun than buying stuff from the comfort of your arm chair and all you need is a telephone and credit card. And boy did Mimi have fun. She bought all kinds of dolls, doll collections, dolls that looked like adults, dolls that were almost the size of adults, dolls of historical figures, etc. Mimi thought that she was always getting a good deal shopping this way, and the dolls were worth much more on the open market. Isn't Home Shopping Channel the open market? At any rate, every room in the house had dolls, some in China Cabinets. The new addition this year was the plastic dust covers that Mimi bought that looked like large sandwich bags. But they did keep the dust off. And the dolls didn't look more weird or scary with the plastic sandwich bags over their heads. The many dolls, paired with her love of watching "Unsolved Mysteries" cranked up loudly on the TV, is the stuff of nightmares. But, at least she had a hobby.

Jocelyn and I left the next day and got home that night. We drove, ate, stopped for gas only and kept on going. We both wanted to sleep in our own beds, smell something besides moth balls and in rooms without scary dolls. And no one told us to make a u-turn on the interstate.

STONE HARBOR

"Mom, can I get my hair done today?" I was 13 and bored in the middle of the summer, looking for something to do. "I can't take you today, but I think that your grandmother is going to have her hair done. Why don't you call and see if she'll take you with her." So that's what I did.

Mimi came and picked me up around 10 and off we went to Stone Harbor. It's about a 20 minute drive from Cape May, and it's also where my grandparents had their summer home and where my parents met. Lots of good memories there. Mimi and I chatted a bit while we rode, and before long we came to some road construction. As the tar-filled gravel started lapping up under the car, Mimi became exasperated. "If that junk is stuck to my car when we get home, I'm going to throw a fit!" I didn't say anything, because that would probably have just made things worse. We rode down Stone Harbor boulevard and on to the next incident.

Stone Harbor Boulevard is a long road that connects Stone Harbor with the mainland. It is a 2-lane road with only a few houses here and there. We rode with the windows open, the breeze blowing in and could smell the marshes. Some folks don't like that smell, but to me it means we're home. As Mimi was recovering from the road incident, a seagull flew directly into the windshield, "AAAAAAAHHHHH!" Mimi screamed, swerved the car, regained her physical composure and to no one in particular started yelling about that bird. "What in the world!" And I started laughing so hard I almost fell out of my seat.. "It's not funny," yelled Mimi. "If that bird had hit the windshield and then gotten into the car it would have a made an awful mess and we could have had a terrible accident." I just laughed harder, knowing full well that I was going to be on Mimi's bad behavior list, or worse, she would pull over and threaten to put me over her knee. Of course by age 10 I was already taller than Mimi. "This is not funny." After the third time, I got myself under control and pretended to be very upset about the bird incident. But honestly I'm still laughing about it.

Finally we arrived at the hair dresser. I wanted to get a perm, after all it was the 1970's and it wasn't my first. I had been getting those since I was at least 5. In those days nobody seemed concerned about kids and chemicals. And Mimi was also getting a perm, so she wouldn't have to wait any longer on me. Now that I think about, I can never remember a time that Mimi did not have her hair permed. So we both got settled into our chairs, I had a magazine and Mimi had her bird story. About 2 hours later we were finished and left the salon, but only one of us was happy. Mimi had a nice perm and it was styled well for her age. I also received a hair cut, a nice perm and it was styled well for a 70-year old. Yes, Mimi and I looked like we were separated at birth, only 50 years apart. I could not believe it! But honestly this made me laugh too, because it was beyond ridiculous. As soon as I got home, I did what you do when you have a bad perm. You try to comb it out and smooth it down with the curling iron and lots of mousse. And you know that eventually it will grow out.

Just a short time ago, my kids and I were shopping at the farmer's market to get a few peaches. My daughter Sydney had just gotten her driver's license, so she drove us home. We were headed down a country road, with the windows open and just enjoying summer. Without any warning, we heard a big thud in the back of the car, as if we had collided with something. Sydney drove the car carefully into a parking lot. We all got out of the car slowly, and left the doors open. And sure enough, there was a dead bird laying on my peaches. The awful mess was all over the inside back window and the headliner. I could not believe it. I guess Mimi is the one laughing now. And no, the bird didn't have a perm, but that would have been perfect.

MOM AND DAD

You know that my parents loved the beach, the ocean, fishing and boating. Nicknamed Cookie and Barracuda as kids, they first met in Stone Harbor, NJ in 1962 and married a year later. Mom's family is from Philadelphia and Dad grew up in Haddon Heights, NJ. During the planning for Mom's funeral Dad shared that they became engaged after only two weeks after they met! And 48 year of marriage later and they still loved the same things. And so it was not surprise that they would raise us at the beach and we are all salt-water fans of the beach and boating

In the late 1970's, Mom and Dad took us to a lake in Connecticut with family friends for vacations. Those were some of the best vacations on the lake. There was a ski boat, a sail boat and a paddle boat that we could use while we were there. And that is where we learned to water ski. They purchased skis for children that were shorter and tied the toes together, making it easier to get up the first time. We were so excited to ski, and to this day, water skiing is one of my favorite things to do. Mom and Dad skied until they were 60, with the same enthusiasm that I expect they had from the beginning. I have a fun memory of skiing with Mom at that lake. We were in the boat and did not see Mom get in the water. We started the engine, slowly pulled away until Mom was ready and then took off. When Mom came out of the water on the skis, she was wearing yellow, inflatable bloomers. We almost had an accident steering the boat in the lake for the laughter. Personal flotation devices came in the form of orange life jackets, vests and belts. But never had we seen the bloomers. Mom found them under the house and put them on when we weren't looking. And when she came out of the water, the look on her face was priceless. Mom knew that she did something hilarious and we responded with hysterical laughter. Mom had a good sense of humor.

Another thing that Mom and Dad did to preserve the family history was their love of the movie camera. Each Christmas morning we would wake up, ask if we could go downstairs, and Mom and Dad would get out the video camera. The camera itself was small. The lights were another story. Looking back on that, I wonder if those are the same lights that they use in jail to make people sit under so that they will tell the truth. Lights, camera, action, and down the stairs we came. With our arms shielding our faces. And then later with our opened presents shielding our faces. I've been watching some of those movies recently and wondering what color our skin really was. Because the movies make us look like we had never seen daylight. Seriously, I appreciate those movies. While watching us as children, and our family members as young adults, I can see my children and even my granddaughter. It is such a gift to see multiple generations and the family characteristics that continue through these generations.

PETS

Every family has a few pets and pet stories. We had a good selection of pets. And I will say that having pets does enhance your life.

DOGS

While I don't remember all of the dogs, I can't remember a time without them. One of our first indoor dogs was Max, who was a mutt that had a little Cocker Spaniel in her mix. We didn't realize that she was a *she* until she had puppies. "Old egg salad" was her nickname because of love of people food, and thus her aroma, but we loved her just the same. She slept at the foot of Laurie's bed, barked at the UPS man, and her own image in the glass of the fire place. We just enjoyed having her around. Max was so good with children and put up with a lot. I remember Mom seeing Max's hair done in Mohawk and then yelling up the stairs "stop moussing the dog's hair." I think that we don't realize how much we love something until it is gone. When Mom and Dad had to put her down right before Thanksgiving 1994, it was devastating. And they vowed no more dogs. Until 2 weeks later when Dad called and said that they had a Lab puppy named Pepper. Pepper was really Dad's dog and in the summer, they swam in the pool after Dad got home from work. After Pepper died the same announcement was made but Dad was easily swayed by dog food commercials. And then Shadow arrived.

CATS

We've never really been indoor cat folks, but seemingly have always had cats around. Even to this day we have outdoor cats at the farm. They've been good hunters, are self-sufficient, and have generally enjoyed sitting on your lap on a pretty day. Or, like our current cat,

Buttercup who is fond of attacking your legs to get some love.

BIRDS

We didn't have birds growing up, but Mom did. She told us about the birds that she raised in Philadelphia as a child. So when it came time to think of a good Christmas present for Mom, of course "bird" came to my mind. We bought the bird and the cage in Virginia, wrapped it up in a towel and drove to New Jersey. When we entered the house, Mom said "that's not a bird is it!" Truthfully, Mom really liked the bird. She named him "Cecil" and hung him in the window in the midst of her favorite view of the pond. (Okay I honestly don't know if it was a him or a her, but there was only one, so no matter). Mom enjoyed Cecil for a few years, even if Pepper barked at him once in a while. Cecil met his demise when Mom and Dad went away and Cecil went to my aunt's house. The story goes that the cat probably lunged at the cage one too many times. Cecil didn't die immediately, but a few days after Mom and Dad returned home. He probably had a weak heart. And maybe that's why we never had indoor cats.

We also had horses, fish and fireflies. Really anything that we could catch in a jar (except the horses).

8

LEGACIES

I know that I have talked a lot about death in this writing, but this time of loss has spawned so many feelings and thoughts that I felt the need to get them all down on paper for my children and other generations. Losing our parents so close together instilled in me the need to record what they had taught us and to preserve for my children, grandchildren, and others to come. Our parents left us with many legacies and I will attempt to share at least some of them with you.

MOM

Today I bought a pizzelle iron. If you're not familiar with that, a pizzelle is a cookie that looks like a waffle. Mom used to tell us about her grandmother from Czechoslovakia making pizzelles on her iron on the stove, one at a time. So Mom taught us all about making Christmas cookies, including pizzelles (Mom's iron made 2 at a time), sprinkling them with powdered sugar and then getting it all over the place when eating them. You know I never remember Mom complaining about the powdered sugar getting everywhere. That must have been her joy.

Mom taught us about legacies early on, before we realized what that meant. Each child, cousin, grandchild and later children-in-law received a hand knitted Christmas stocking with our name on it. Mine was the first, and my parents had a photo with me in the stocking for my first Christmas. When each grandchild was born, Mom would cross-stitch a baby quilt, each one unique and never replicated. Legacies for Mom were food and home. When Mom was in rehabilitation to build up her strength that the cancer had taken from her, at Christmas she asked if I would take on the knitting responsibilities. I agreed, provided she would help me. We didn't get that chance to work together one more time. But a friend recently sat by my side while I worked on a stocking for the last grandchild. I had been working on this for a year, and will tell you only about the first 6 attempts to get it right. I thought about throwing in the towel several times, but this was honestly the only thing that Mom asked of me. So for an hour and a half, my friend sat by my side, watched me knit and gently guided me along. For a moment it was like Mom was with me again. I hope my friend knows how much that time meant to me. This isn't just a knitted Christmas stocking, it was Mom's legacy that I am doing my best to preserve and pass on.

Mom's best dishes were roast turkey and Jewish apple cake. Laurie pipes in here to add galumpkis (aka stuffed cabbage leaves). Dad loved turkey and we all enjoyed waking up to the smell of the turkey that Mom put in the oven the night before Thanksgiving. My favorite part was when the turkey came out of the oven, I would break off the crunchy part of the stuffing and eat it before Dad started carving. Delicious! My mouth is watering now just thinking about it. That smell of turkey today is a good memory. And the Jewish apple cake people still ask for. A cousin of ours sent me some pictures from Mom's childhood recently. In the middle of the one of the pictures was that cake, 40-50 years ago! I make this at least once a year. And when we celebrate Thanksgiving next week with Laurie and her family, the cake will be right in the middle of the table. Next to the turkey, of course.

DAD

One of Dad's qualities was his humility. He never bragged and gave endlessly and oftentimes anonymously to people in the community. Police Captain Brian Marker presented a Community Partnership Award to Dad in 2009 for assisting the police department with calls where there was a death, and also for sponsoring numerous community projects. I can't remember Dad ever mentioning this. .

He helped everyone. Dad delivered deliver "Meals on Wheels" to the residents of Lower Township in between funerals. Holidays at the Evoy house always included a full table. Besides his own the 5 of us children, Dad often invited people who didn't have a family to spend the holidays with. It could be a young man in the Coast Guard away from home for the first time or the elderly friend in the church who didn't have family near by. As the head of the Mission's Committee at Tabernacle UMC, Dad led annual mission trips to minister to the less fortunate in the Appalachian Mountains in Kentucky at the Red Bird and Henderson Settlements. He and Mom made Christmas brighter for needy children in Camden by bringing them vanloads of toys. Another project near and dear to Dad's heart was the Melmark Center, a home for severely handicapped children. His final project was repairing the historic church on the grounds of Covenant Presbyterian Church. Although he didn't live to see its completion, his name will remain there as the Wyn Evoy Sr. Community Center.

When Dad became ill and died, it almost seemed unbearable after losing Mom such a short time earlier. However, I felt that God had given me the strength to speak at Dad's funeral and let others know that we had learned from him and were willing to work to preserve Dad's legacy. I leave you with his eulogy.

WYN EVOY TRIBUTE

On behalf of the Evoy family I want to thank you for coming. We are trying to understand why Dad has been taken from us at this time. Over the last few days we have tried to imagine the good that can come from this. And the thought that came to mind was the great legacy that Dad has left behind.

If I had to describe the things that matter to him most they are God, family, friends and country. Dad took us to church. He took us to Sunday school. And all through our lives he has passed on his wisdom. We watched his faith grow. And while Dad could hold a conversation with anyone, his actions and living example has spoken volumes to us. We didn't always get it at the time. But in recent years I have had many conversations where something happened and I had to tell Dad that he was right all along. He would laugh, but I knew he was glad that I understood.

Our Dad was a great son, husband, brother, father and friend. He loved his family and friends. One thing that stood out in my mind is his desire to help others. And not because he was asked but because he had a huge, compassionate heart, and could see a need and solve a problem. This is certainly part of his legacy that we will not only carry on, but pass on to future generations.

And finally, Dad taught us to love our country. I can never remember a day when the flag of our great country did not fly in front of the funeral home. Dad taught us to raise and lower the flag without allowing it to touch the ground. He showed us how to properly fold a flag with stars up on the outside. Of course on windy days we would lower the flag, grab and end and let it whip us around the pole. While we didn't think Dad was looking, I'm sure he knew what we were doing, but also that we were learning.

How would I describe Dad? A verse kept coming to my mind over the past few days.

Galations 5:22, "But the fruit of the spirit is Love, Joy, Peace, Patience, Kindness, Goodness, Faithfulness, Gentleness, and Self-Control" Dad embodies all of these. And I have to believe that when Dad walked through the gates of Heaven, that he would hear, "Well done good and faithful servant."

We love you Dad. We'll miss you. But we will carry on the gift of legacy that you left behind.

9

50 YEARS OF LEARNING

. . . .

I am so thankful for these first 50 years of my life. And while I have learned much during these decades, there is still more to learn. Much more. When I narrowed it down, these are the things that mean the most to me, and not necessarily in this order: perspective, love, forgiveness, gratefulness.

Perspective – I wish that I had been born with the perspective that I have today. My sister says that this is one my favorite words. But it's true, when you gain perspective about any situation, you can pinpoint the actual truths about others, God's truths, and then can move forward accordingly. I've been teaching a youth Sunday school for a few years (and continue to learn through teaching). But this is one of those times when things become so clear. To see things through the eyes of someone young, just starting out in life. I believe that this is one of the ways that God helps us to grow. As a teen, we see things narrowly, things that affect us, our family, our friends. But as I've aged, God has opened my eyes to the bigger picture. One of the ways for me, is how to deal with death. Our family has dealt with a great amount of illness and death in the last three years, starting with the loss of our mother. While we were making plans for her funeral and later plans for our father's funeral, God reminded me that our loss was not ours alone. Mom and Dad had other family members, close friends, co-workers, church family and a community that was also grieving. They worked with our parents daily, saw them weekly and when Mom and Dad were gone, a big hole was also left in their hearts. It helped me to deal with their loss (which is an ongoing process) to help to comfort others. Someone whose example left a big impact on me is our step-mother. She lost her first husband at a young age and was left to raise young children on her own. But at her husband's funeral, I saw Marie comforting others. That's right, comforting others. That has to be a God directed action. Because she knew Jesus as her Lord and savior, she was prepared with whatever life had in store and how to act in a Godly manner. Perspective. It's not just about me.

Love – I have to admit that through college and my early years of marriage and child rearing, I strayed away from church. But eventually I came back. God drew me to him and I listened and really learned about love. Loving others unconditionally. I think that this really starts when you have children. And then when you are in church, listening the sermon, thinking about how you should work on yourself, it finally dawns on you that you have been love unconditionally; by your parents first, family, friends and church. I felt so loved in church when I came to one as a divorced mother of two children. The congregation did not question my past, only looked to my future. They lifted me up, educated my children and welcomed us all with open arms. It has to be a taste of what heaven will be like when we meet Jesus. With all of that love coming our way, how can we not pass it on to others.

Forgiveness – If I have learned anything during my time on earth it is that life is short and can be taken away at any moment. So I don't have time for ugly. Anger, holding grudges, and withholding forgiveness can be ugly and is not part of God's plan for me. Perspective has helped me with this, making it easier to forgive. When we are in the middle of something unpleasant, I have to take a hard look at the situation and ask a few questions. What is the intention of the other party? Do they know the difference between right and wrong? Are they capable of making the right decision? Who is influencing their decisions? What will our relationship be going forward? The last question is the most important – relationship. I do not believe in forgive and forget. I believe in forgive and don't make the same mistake going forward. We never really forget, we move forward without the burden of reminding ourselves of the perceived offense. I say perceived, because remember the first question is not as important as the last. And finally what does God want? His desire is all that matters. And when forgiveness comes, healing begins.

Gratefulness – Without getting too sappy, I really am grateful for all the good in my life and recognized that this could only come from God. I am grateful for the people in life. And I am so grateful for joy and laughter. My Aunt Marty says "never lose your sense of humor." She's a great example of that, sees humor in everyday things and always willing to hear my funny stories too. I have a friend that from time-to-time asks "want to hear a funny story" and my response is "always." I hope that when it is time to leave this earth, my family and friends will be sitting around telling funny stories, the kind that makes tears run down your face and hold on so your insides don't burst out. Laughter is one of the best things about my life. I'm so grateful.

EPILOGUE

Why would I be writing this book at this point in time? Well, life is short, very short. This has become real to me over the last few years. I don't want to wait to tell the stories that I want the children to know, to share the legacies of my parents and to speak to those that may not know the Lord, Jesus Christ. Because of Him, I have been able to face whatever has come my way (not always gracefully), but here I sit, already lived a lifetime. I want others to know how grateful I am for

God, family, friends, church family and community. And for those who do not know God, I share this:

What I believe – The Apostles Creed - http://www.umc.org/what-we-believe/apostles-creed -traditional-ecumenical

I believe in God, the Father Almighty,
maker of heaven and earth;
And in Jesus Christ his only Son, our Lord;
who was conceived by the Holy Spirit,
born of the Virgin Mary,
suffered under Pontius Pilate,
was crucified, dead, and buried;*
the third day he rose from the dead;
he ascended into heaven,
and sitteth at the right hand of
God the Father Almighty;
from thence he shall come to judge
the quick and the dead.
I believe in the Holy Spirit,

the holy catholic** church,
the communion of saints,
the forgiveness of sins,
the resurrection of the body,
and the life everlasting. Amen.

If you don't believe, would you at least consider that God has a plan for your life.

Romans 8:28
And we know that in all things God works
for the good of those who love him, who have
been called according to his purpose.

If you don't believe, would you at least consider that following Jesus Christ is freeing, not limiting.

John 8:32
"Then you will know the truth, and
the truth will set you free."

If you don't believe, would you at least consider that God wants you and I want you to have what I have, "peace that passes all understanding" while I'm on earth and "eternal life" John 3:16 beyond this world.

Philippians 4:7
"And the peace of God,
which transcends all understanding, will guard
your hearts and your minds in Christ Jesus."

John 3:16
"For God so loved the world that he gave his
one and only Son, that whoever believes in
him shall not perish but have eternal life."

This last one is the one that has pulled me through the darkest times. Even in death, I believe in my heart and mind that this is not the end, but "until we meet again." Life is hard enough, and harder without God's peace.

I can't say that I have any grand accomplishments in my life. But I have certainly been blessed by God and grateful that He has given me the strength, mercy, grace, and forgiveness that I need but have not earned. I laugh with my friends over things that happen and have said that when I die, on my gravestone I would like it to say "at least she tried." This would be a good way to describe my cooking skills, craft attempts, vacation adventures and many other things that we do in life. A few years ago, we attended a church that was dedicating a new building, and the minister asked us to write our favorite bible verse on the cement floor in permanent marker. Once the carpet was installed, those verses would forever be there. I wrote "Love Never Fails" from I Corinthians 13.8. God's love NEVER fails. That's really what I want on my gravestone.

Printed in the United States
By Bookmasters